God Is Awesome

Robin Prince Monroe
Illustrated by Marlene McAuley

Concordia Publishing House

For Mom and Dad
I love you so much!

God is the biggest.

He is bigger than the tallest building

Psalm 48:1–3

or the grandest mountain.

Psalm 97:5

He is even bigger than the gigantic, blue sky.

Psalm 104:2–3

In fact He made the gigantic, blue sky.

Psalm 19:1

God is the strongest.

He is stronger than the mightiest elephant

Job 40:15–19

or the most powerful bulldozer.

He is even stronger than the fiercest storm.

Psalm 29:7

God is the smartest.

He is smarter than my teacher.

Job 38:36

He is even smarter than the president and the president's computer.

Psalm 47:8–9

Did you know God knows everything?
EVERYTHING!
Even Daddy doesn't know everything.

Hebrews 4:13

God is the best.

He is perfect.
He NEVER, EVER makes a mistake.

Sometimes I make a mistake.
Then I say, "I'm sorry."

Romans 3:23–24

Some mistakes I can fix with my eraser.
I bet God's pencils don't have erasers.

God is the most loving.
He sent His Son, Jesus, to give His life for me.

He loves me more than my best friend loves me—
more than Grandma loves me.
He even loves me more than my mom and dad love me.

John 3:16

Did you know God is love? My table is wood.
My bowl is glass. My ball is plastic.

And . . . God is love.

1 John 4:16

God is

THE BIGGEST,

THE STRONGEST,

THE SMARTEST,

THE BEST,

THE MOST LOVING.

GOD IS AWESOME!

Psalm 86:10

Dear Parent:

Your child will have a natural love for "est" words—the *tallest* tree, the *biggest* ice-cream cone, the *fastest* rocket. As you enjoy this book find similar examples of big, strong, smart things in your child's world. Together, thank God for being even greater. He loves you and your child so much that He sent His own Son to give His life for you. God is awesome!